My Pretty Pink Bible Sticker Bag

Have fun completing the sticker and colouring activities! Pull out the sticker sheets and keep them by you when you complete each sticker activity page. Have fun!

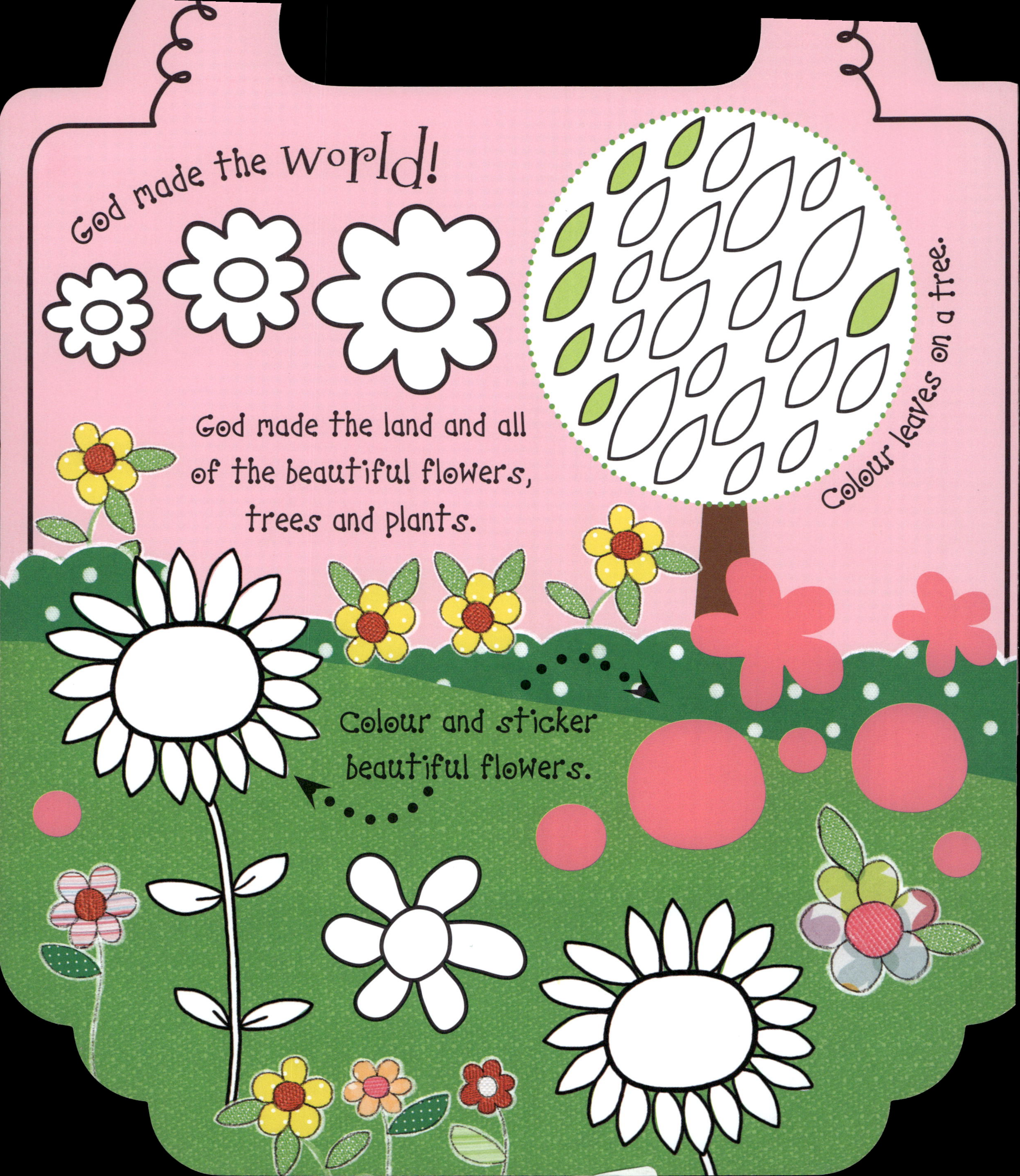

God made the world!

God made the land and all of the beautiful flowers, trees and plants.

Colour leaves on a tree.

Colour and sticker beautiful flowers.

God made the daytime!

Sticker friends having fun in the park.

God made the night-time!

Colour a bear to cuddle in the dark.

God made the animals, from big cats to small, fluffy cats!

Find the missing animal stickers.

Colour Pony and sticker her missing apples.

Decorate the frame with heart and star stickers.

Draw your favourite animal in the frame.

God made all the fish that swim in the sea.

Use your stickers to complete the fish patterns.

Colour and decorate the fish.

A snake tempted Adam and Eve to eat the fruit from God's forbidden tree.

Sticker apples on the tree.

Colour the snake.

God told Noah to build a **big boat** called an **ark!**

Colour the **ark.**

Noah took his family and two of each animal into the ark to keep them safe.

Sticker Noah and the missing sheep.

Colour and sticker food for the ark.

sticker Noah's missing animals.

All of the animals went into the ark, both big and small!

Colour the elephant.

Find stickers for the missing animals.

God made it rain and rain. Soon the Earth was covered in water!

Sticker raindrops.

Sticker more fish in the sea.

Make Mother Bunny nice and warm in the ark.

Decorate her blanket with flower and heart stickers!

Sticker 2 baby bunnies.

The rain stopped and the ark found dry land!

Sticker the missing animals.

God sent a beautiful rainbow as a promise that He would not flood the Earth again.

Colour God's rainbow in the sky.

Sticker animals playing in the sun.

Joseph had a special coat that his father gave him.

His brothers were very jealous. They wanted special coats too!

Make Joseph's coat bright and colourful.

Sticker more playful rabbits.

Do you have some very special things?

Draw and colour them here.

Draw something special in this box.

Colour and decorate the special dress.

Add a pattern to the shoes.

Joseph was put in prison in Egypt. He explained the dreams people had.

Seven fat cows meant seven years when they could grow lots of food.

Sticker the missing cows.

Seven thin cows meant
seven years of famine,
when they could grow
very little food.

Colour the thin cows.

Joseph helped the people of Egypt
store food for the famine.

One day, an Egyptian princess found Baby Moses by the river.

The princess took Moses
and looked after him as if
he was her own son.

Find the missing stickers.

God spoke to Moses from a burning bush.

Moses led God's people out of slavery in Egypt.

Colour the burning bush.

Sticker a staff for Moses.

David was a shepherd boy. He was very brave.

He protected his father's sheep from lions, wolves and other wild animals.

Colour a fierce lion.

David's people were fighting the Philistines!

Goliath was a
tall, strong
Philistine soldier.

David put a
stone in his sling,
and hurled it at
Goliath.

Find the missing stickers.

David's stone hit Goliath between the eyes and he fell down dead!

The Philistines ran away.

Use your stickers to decorate Goliath's shield and sword.

Do you sometimes get scared?
Trust God, and ask him to look after you.

Woof!
Woof!

Sticker dogs scaring the kittens on the wall.

Colour this cute kitten.

Sticker more hungry mice!

An angel came to Mary and gave her amazing news.
"You will have a very special baby. He will be the son of God."
Colour a beautiful angel.

Mary gave birth to Jesus in a stable.

Draw and colour Jesus' bed.

Use your stickers to finish the animal patterns.

A special star shone over the stable in Bethlehem.

Draw and colour this amazing star.

Sticker stars too!

An angel appeared to shepherds in a bright light.

She told them to go to Bethlehem, where God's special king had been born in a stable.

Sticker more sheep on the hill.

Three Wise men followed the bright star to find Jesus.

Colour the three gifts and decorate them with stickers.

All of the animals gathered around the baby Jesus.

Colour the stable and the animals.

Jesus grew up to be a wise man and he performed miracles!

Colour the fish.

Jesus fed thousands of people with only a few fish and loaves of bread. People were amazed. This was a great miracle.

Sticker the missing loaves!

God gives us lots of food to enjoy.

Draw your favourite meal on the plate.

Colour the drink.

Draw your favourite treats in the jars.

Sticker more yummy treats.

Jesus died so that we can be God's friends.

Draw your best friend in this picture frame.

Sticker more best friends.

Draw a group of friends in this picture frame.

God loves you.
You are special.

Draw a picture of yourself.

Draw things you love to do in here.

Use stickers to decorate the pictures.

God gives us our family to love and care for us.

Draw your family at home.

Sticker balls for the dogs to play with.

Where in the world do you live?

Write your answer on the flag.

Write the town you live in here.

....

....

Draw your house here.

Jesus' birthday is on Christmas day.

When is your birthday?

....

....

Colour the cake and presents, then decorate them with stickers.

sticker candles on the birthday cake!

Page 9
Page 11
Pages 12 and 13
Page 14

Page 15
Pages 16 and 17
Page 18

Page 18
Page 19
Page 20

Page 22
Page 25
Page 26
Page 23

Page 26
Page 27
Page 29
Pages 30 and 31

Page 32
Page 34
Page 35
Pages 36 and 37

Page 38
Page 40
Extra stickers!

My Pretty Pink Bible Sticker Bag

Pretty pink pages packed full of Bible sticker activities to complete and colour.

make believe ideas ltd
The Wilderness, Berkhamsted, Hertfordshire, HP4 2AZ, UK.

Manufactured in China.
www.makebelieveideas.com

Designed by Chris Scollen. Illustrations by Lara Ede.

Parental Guidance

Promotes hand-eye coordination

Stimulates imaginative play

3+ YEARS

ISBN13: 978-1-86024-844-3
9 781860 248443
www.authenticmedia.co.uk

Authentic

09201604